ECONOMICS and

THE MORAL ORDER

ECONOMICS and THE MORAL ORDER

by

JOSEPH BALDACCHINO

INTRODUCTION BY RUSSELL KIRK

NATIONAL HUMANITIES INSTITUTE
WASHINGTON, D.C.

FIRST PRINTING — MARCH 1985
SECOND PRINTING — APRIL 1989

ISBN 0-932783-00-7
Library of Congress Catalog Card No. 84-062819

The NATIONAL HUMANITIES INSTITUTE is a tax exempt organization that promotes theoretically significant research, publication and teaching in the humanities, including the social sciences properly conceived. It seeks to contribute to the reinvigoration and development of the principles upon which Western civilization is based.

NATIONAL HUMANITIES INSTITUTE
214 Massachusetts Avenue, N.E.
Suite 470
Washington, D.C. 20002
(202) 544-3158

Contents

Introduction by Russell Kirk 9

I. The Insufficiency of Economics 13

II. The Economic Dimension of Morality 23

III. Economics as Means to Morality 29

Index 42

Introduction

Economics moves upwards into politics, and politics upwards into ethics — so Irving Babbitt wrote. Mr. Baldacchino's admirable study on economics and the moral order explains systematically this truth.

Permit me to illustrate the point by an anecdote that Wilhelm Röpke, that eminent citizen of Geneva, related to me a quarter of a century ago.

During the Second World War, the city of Geneva allocated garden plots to such of its citizens — particularly of the working class — as desired to cultivate their own vegetables in a time of food-scarcity. These plots were situated on public lands along the line of the long-demolished ramparts of Geneva. Erecting little tool-sheds here and there, Genevans were able to grow much of their own food and to have the pleasure of fruitful outdoor exercise. This gardening became so popular that Geneva's magistrates extended the privilege after the end of the war.

Presently Ludwig von Mises came to visit Röpke at Geneva. Röpke took his guest to inspect the garden allotments, an example of Röpke's "Third Way" in economic concerns.

Mises shook his head disapprovingly. "A very inefficient way of producing foodstuffs," he observed.

"But," Röpke replied, "perhaps a very efficient way of producing human happiness."

Just so. Economic productivity is made for man, not man for economic productivity. Those who ignore humankind's moral nature in their economic calculations are condemned to fall under the domination of squalid oligarchs professing some merciless New Morality.

A free and prosperous economy is the by-product, so to speak, of a society influenced by sound moral principles and accustomed to good moral habits. Some people would like to separate economics from morals; but they are unable to do so. For unless most men and women recognize some sort of moral order, an economy cannot function except in a small and precarious way.

All human creations and institutions are connected with moral ideas and habits. Concepts of right and wrong haunt us in everything we do. Production, trading, saving, and the whole economic apparatus depend upon general morality. If moral habits are lacking, the only other way to produce goods is by compulsion — by what is called servile labor.

Any economy that functions well relies upon a high degree of *honesty*. In the market, buyers and sellers must be able to trust one another ordinarily. Any advanced economy is based upon contracts: agreements to sell and to buy, promises to pay, deeds of sale, all sorts of commercial instruments. Many commercial contracts are oral, rather than written. Procedures at a public auction suggest the necessity for honesty in bidding and payment. On a much larger scale, the complex apparatus of stock markets depends on such implicit contracts — and on ordinary honesty.

On the other hand, those societies in which theft, cheating, and lying are common do not ordinarily develop successful economies. If production and distribution can be carried on only under armed protection and without certainty of payment, little will be produced and distributed, above the level of bare subsistence.

Another moral quality or habit important for the success of an economy is the custom of doing good work — of producing goods of high quality. The Romans had a word for this: *industria*, a moral virtue from which our English word industry is derived. Goods should be produced, and services rendered, for the sake of turning out something satisfactory or even admirable — not for the sake of cash payment merely. This belief in working faithfully and well is connected with the virtue called *charity*. For charity is not a handout, primarily; the word means tenderness or love, affection for other people. The producer who creates first-rate goods is serving other people, and can take satisfaction in that service.

One more virtue of the marketplace is a kind of courage: what the old Romans called *fortitude*. This economic courage includes the willingness to take risks; the ability to endure hard times; the talent to hold out against all the disappointments, ingratitude, and folly that fall upon people in the world of getting and spending.

And as moral habits sustain an economy, so vicious habits undermine an economy. In particular, the vice of *envy* can destroy general prosperity. In Marxist lands, envy is approved by the men in power. Private wealth and personal success are denounced on principle. The Marxist indoctrinator deliberately preaches envy. By appealing to that strong vice, he may be able to pull down constitutions, classes, religions, and economic systems. Because the competitive market brings substantial success to a good many individuals, the Marxist hates the market. A consistent Marxist declares that when two people exchange goods in a market, both are cheated. Yes, *both* — that is what the Marxist says. Exchange itself is "capitalist oppression," the Marxist propagandist proclaims. Certainly little profitable exchange survives in Communist countries. Envying the market's popularity and success, the Marxist furiously denounces the market.

The opposite of the vice called envy is the virtue called *generosity*. This too is a moral quality upon which a sound economy depends. Producer and consumer, when moved by generosity, do not envy one another: they may be competitors, but they are friendly competitors, like contestants in some sport. Generosity brings admiration of the achievements and qualities of others. Like the other virtues, generosity grows out of the soil of a healthy general moral order.

Any society's moral order develops from its religion, its philosophy, its humane literature. The discipline of political economy, little understood until the latter half of the eighteenth century, is no independent creation: what economic views one holds must depend upon one's apprehension of human nature. An economic system indifferent to morality will not long endure. For proof of these theses, read with attention Mr. Baldacchino's succinct study, the work of a sound scholar endowed with a philosophical habit of mind.

—*Russell Kirk*

I

The Insufficiency of Economics

It is widely acknowledged that the economic system shared by the United States and other Western democracies, and most commonly called "capitalism" or the "free-market system," [1] has created a higher level of affluence within a context of broad personal liberty for greater numbers of people than any other economic arrangement in history. Yet for all its manifest accomplishments, the free-enterprise system cannot long survive the highly emotional assault waged against it by Marxists and other proponents of collectivist planning unless it is also seen as at least potentially compatible with man's ethical nature.

One of the few leading scholarly defenders of the market economy in this century to emphasize the capitalist system's subordination to — and ultimate dependence on — a higher political and ethical order was the late economist

---

1. While such terms as "capitalism" or "socialism" denote merely pragmatic classifications and therefore are necessarily somewhat arbitrary, what is here meant by capitalism is a system based to a significant extent on the voluntary exchange of goods and services, private ownership of the means of production, and the free play of prices in response to supply and demand.

and social thinker Wilhelm Röpke. It is a "fatal misconception," wrote Röpke many years ago, to believe, as a popular notion has it, that

> Communism is a weed particular to the marshes of poverty and capable of being eradicated by an improvement in the standard of living.... Surely everyone must know by now that the world war against Communism cannot be won with radio sets, refrigerators, and wide-screen films. It is not a contest for a better supply of goods — unfortunately for the free world, whose record in this field cannot be beaten. The truth is that it is a profound, all-encompassing conflict of two ethical systems in the widest sense, a struggle for the very conditions of man's spiritual and moral existence.[2]

According to Röpke, the free world's economic system is most accurately viewed as an essential (though subordinate) *part* of a wider political and moral order: a part whose fate is inextricably tied to the ethical and cultural health of Western civilization as a whole.[3]

If Röpke is correct in his view that "people do not live by cheaper vacuum cleaners alone"[4] and that an economic system without at least a potential for serving man's ethical nature contains the seeds of its own disintegration, then it seemingly would behoove the advocates of capitalism to make every effort to demonstrate its moral worth as well as its efficiency, important though the latter may be. Indeed, one would expect them to make this effort if for no other reason than to counter the telling effect with which the foes of free enterprise have repeated Marx's assertion that capitalism leaves "no other nexus between man and man than naked self-interest," drowning all higher values "in the icy

---

2. Wilhelm Röpke, *A Humane Economy: The Social Framework of the Free Market* (Indianapolis: Liberty Fund, 1971), 103.

3. Ernest van den Haag more recently has made the same point in a slightly different context. He notes: "People will tolerate a social or economic system, however efficient, only if they perceive it as just." See Ernest van den Haag, ed. *Capitalism: Sources of Hostility* (New Rochelle, N.Y.: Epoch Books for the Heritage Foundation, 1979), 19.

4. Röpke, *Humane Economy*, 107.

water of egotistical calculation." [5] Yet, ironically, those twentieth-century economic thinkers who have most brilliantly and painstakingly shown the superior efficiency of the free-market system have often done much to undermine its essential moral foundation by denying the very existence of a transcendent moral obligation.

A prime example is Ludwig von Mises. A giant among history's economic scholars, Mises has yet to receive the full recognition which is his due. Just one of many accomplishments was his pioneering demonstration, in 1922, that the economic calculation necessary for an efficient allocation of resources is impossible in the absence of free markets and private ownership of property.[6] But to the all-important further question — efficiency for what purpose? — Mises replies that questions of morality, of good and evil, are beyond the reach of philosophic inquiry. He writes:

> The teachings of praxeology [his term for the science of human action] and economics are valid for every human action without regard to its underlying motives, causes, and goals. The ultimate judgments of value and the ultimate ends of human action are given for any kind of scientific inquiry; they are not open to any further analysis. Praxeology deals with the ways and means chosen for the attainment of such ultimate ends. Its object is means, not ends.[7]

Mises goes on to speak of "the subjectivism of the general science of human action. It takes the ultimate ends chosen by acting man as data, it is entirely neutral with regard to them, and it refrains from passing any value judgments." [8]
Another renowned free-market economist who will not

5. Karl Marx and Friedrich Engels, *The Manifesto of the Communist Party*, in *The Essential Left* (New York: Barnes & Noble, 1961), 17.

6. See Ludwig von Mises, *Socialism: An Economic and Sociological Analysis*, trans. J. Kahane (London: Jonathan Cape, 1951).

7. Ludwig von Mises, *Human Action: A Treatise on Economics* (Chicago: Regnery, 1966), 21.

8. *Ibid.*

acknowledge any universal moral purpose is Nobel-laureate Friedrich A. Hayek. Like Mises, Hayek believes questions of good and evil to be beyond the scope of philosophic investigation. Rather, justice or morality resides in the observance of abstract and somewhat arbitrary rules which "are *treated*...as absolute values" because they have been found by long experience to "increase the opportunities for unknown persons" to serve their own particular ends.[9]

In line with this general approach, Hayek describes the free-market economy as a "game" of skill and chance governed by abstract rules. Within the context of these rules, the self-interest of each "player" dictates that he make "the highest worthwhile contribution to the common pool from which each will win an uncertain share." A "worthwhile contribution" is, for Hayek, whatever will help others to serve their own particularistic self-interest.[10]

The trouble with such theories is that they are incomplete. Though claiming to give a full description of human action, or will,[11] they fail to consider the possibility of different qualities or categories of will, though it can be argued that the existence of these distinct categories is a matter of direct experience. As a result, the ethical dimension of human life — more specifically, the existence of a transcendent moral standard that can be known philosophically (i.e., without recourse to special revelation or dogma) — is entirely missed. As we shall see later, this in turn leads to a highly exaggerated view of what can be expected from economics alone.

One American writer who for more than a generation has warned against placing economics at the height of human aspiration is the scholar and man of letters Russell

---

9. F. A. Hayek, *The Mirage of Social Justice*, Vol. II of *Law, Legislation and Liberty* (Chicago: University of Chicago Press, 1976), 12–23; emphasis added.

10. F. A. Hayek, *New Studies in Philosophy, Politics, Economics and the History of Ideas* (Chicago: University of Chicago Press, 1978), 60; 62.

11. See Mises, *Human Action*, 13.

Kirk. Beginning in the late 1940s, Kirk objected to the ethical deficiency of economistic liberalism, as exemplified by Mises and, to a lesser extent, Hayek. In contrast to the view that self-interest alone provides sufficient cement for the social order, Kirk insisted that the market has its place but that it must be joined by an elevation of character synonymous with what Aristotle called "friendship" and Christians call "love of neighbor."

The wise man, Kirk noted, "does not believe that the end or aim of life is competition; or success; or enjoyment; or longevity; or power; or possessions. He believes, instead, that the object of life is Love." [12] Kirk pointed to Röpke as a way out, and was largely responsible for introducing the German writer to an American audience. More recently, Kirk has described the contemporary disciples of nineteenth-century liberalism, known as libertarians, as "chirping sectaries" having a thoroughly misguided view of human nature.[13] But despite Kirk's strong and persistent urging that the ethical shortcomings of *laissez-faire* doctrine be overcome, very little philosophical investigation of the problems involved has yet been done.[14]

Among those who have addressed these issues and provided a philosophical basis for the needed work are Irving Babbitt, Paul Elmer More, Benedetto Croce, and — more recently — Folke Leander and Claes G. Ryn. Babbitt and More have identified the existence within the human breast of two competing elements of will: the lower will, which is manifested in the merely selfish desires, and the higher will, which is experienced as a propensity to put a check on those

12. Russell Kirk, *A Program for Conservatives* (rev. ed.; Chicago: Regnery, 1962), 18.

13. Russell Kirk, "Libertarians: the Chirping Sectaries," *Modern Age*, XXV (Fall 1981).

14. One who has recently taken impressive steps in this direction is Michael Novak. See e.g. *The Spirit of Democratic Capitalism* (New York: Simon & Schuster, 1982).

desires in favor of a more deeply satisfying goal known to be good for its own sake.[15]

Both elements of will are capable of establishing a certain unity of action within the personality, but only the ethical will can bring men together in true community. An individual who is intent upon serving nothing more than his own narrow self-interest or that of some group with which he identifies himself will not necessarily follow every passing whim. He is more likely to put prudential checks on his impulses. Before acting, he will consider the probable consequences of allowing a given impulse to pass into fruition; and if the results, anticipated in the imagination, seem inimical to his goals or those of his group, he will look for another course of action conducive to more agreeable consequences. In this way, selfish interest alone (i.e., the lower will) can lead men to impose a kind of prudential self-discipline on themselves, and it may even lead them to unite with others in a kind of group discipline intended to avoid the war of all against all.[16]

As Ryn has observed, however, such merely expedient group discipline and the social peace towards which it aspires "will be highly precarious and ultimately succumb to the centrifugal forces of partisan wills" unless there is "recognition of an ethical, that is, self-justifying, goal above competing interests." [17] Referring to the higher will as the ethical conscience, Ryn defines it as "the awareness, stronger in some people than in others, that there is a sacred purpose to human life which transcends the transitory biases of individuals and peoples, and which can be vio-

15. See Irving Babbitt, *Democracy and Leadership* (Indianapolis: Liberty Classics, 1979). Also see Paul Elmer More, "Definitions of Dualism," in *The Drift of Romanticism*, Vol. VIII of *Shelburne Essays* (11 vols.; New York: Phaeton Press, 1967).

16. See Folke Leander, *The Inner Check: A Concept of Paul Elmer More with Reference to Benedetto Croce* (London: Edward Wright, 1974), 13–16.

17. Claes G. Ryn, *Democracy and the Ethical Life: A Philosophy of Politics and Community* (Baton Rouge: Louisiana State University Press, 1978), 81.

lated only at the price of a loss of meaning and worth." [18]
Like the lower will, the higher will puts a check on impulses
that would conflict with its purpose. The difference is that,
while the lower will values some form of arbitrary self-
indulgence, the ethical conscience values what is simultaneously the good for the individual and the good for all,
namely the universal good for man. Hence man's ethical
conscience is experienced as a check on merely selfish purposes or, put another way, a check on the lower or arbitrary
will.

Mises gives an excellent account of the power of what is
here described as the lower will to restrain some impulses
while approving others, thereby giving a certain coherence
to human action.[19] But though he also recognizes that his-
torians can "establish the facts that people were motivated
by definite value judgments," [20] and that it is possible, at
least with regard to theoretical actions (i.e., actions having
truth as their immanent telos), to distinguish between acts
that are "arbitrary" or "ill-intentioned" and those which
are not,[21] he fails to draw the obvious conclusion that arbitrary actions and those that are not arbitrary belong to fun-
damentally different categories and that this difference is
open to philosophical investigation.

Given man's dualistic nature, it must be recognized that
narrowly selfish interest will always play a large part in
social and political life. Normally, Ryn observes, the best
that statesmen can hope for is, by framing good laws and
other social structures, to enlist self-interest in the service
of moral ends. But, he cautions:

> Lest the influence of ethical motives in politics be
> entirely discounted, it should also be noted that in a
> society where men are growing insensitive to the
> demands of the ethical life, their enlightened self-

18. *Ibid.*, 8.
19. Mises, *Human Action*, 16–17.
20. *Ibid.*, 55.
21. See e.g. *Ibid.*, 15, 54.

interest, too, will be increasingly difficult to discern. As their ethical vision is blurred, there is less to restrain their cruder inclinations. Men will become more indiscriminate in their choice of ends and means. The power struggle, which before was leavened somewhat by the ethical pull, will get harsher. Whereas ethical conscience, the will to the common good, used to give to the constitution and to the laws generally an aura of dignity which made it easier for the citizens to recognize allegiance to the lawful order as being in their long-term self-interest, they are now going to look at the laws with less reverence and not be as predisposed against breaking them, if it would serve their own immediate goals and go undetected. In that sense, it may be said that any civilized political order is ultimately rooted in ethical conscience.[22]

Against this backdrop, we can now return to Hayek's view that ours is an "open and abstract society, in which an order results from individuals observing the same abstract rules of the game while using their own knowledge in the pursuit of their own ends." [23] We have seen that this is true up to a point. But Hayek takes it for granted that the "players" in the game of free market will obey the rules. What is not clear is why, if those rules have no higher value than their usefulness in fulfilling the arbitrary self-interest of unknown others, anyone would obey them if his own immediate selfish interest could be enhanced either by cheating or by using political muscle to force a change in the rules.

An answer that is often given is one used by John Stuart Mill, who argued that happiness understood as mere individual pleasure "is a good; that each person's happiness is a good to that person; and the general happiness, therefore, a good to the aggregate of all persons." [24] But though

---

22. Ryn, *Democracy and the Ethical Life*, 24–25.

23. Hayek, *New Studies*, 61.

24. See Mill, *Utilitarianism*, in *The Philosophy of John Stuart Mill*, ed. Marshall Cohen (New York: Modern Library, 1961), 363.

this is correct as far as it goes, Mill errs in inferring that, because maximization of the general happiness (understood as the aggregate of individual pleasures) is desired by the aggregate of *all* persons, it necessarily follows that the general happiness will be desired by *each* person. The trouble with this argument, as More points out,[25] is that the "feeling of pleasure and pain is the sense of the increase or diminution of our individual life. In so far as the pleasure of another may result in activities beneficial to ourselves, or create the expectation of similar pleasure in ourselves, and thus enlarges our sense of life, it may awaken sympathetic pleasure in us.... But, on the contrary, the pleasure of another is equally capable of awakening an antipathetic pain in us, when it means an activity in the other that is detrimental to us and diminishes our sense of life...." It is only when man has reorganized his purposes so that he wills the "universal end" common to all as his own individual end that he moves into true harmony with his fellow men; and it is the feeling that accompanies this partial transcending of the ego which is true happiness.[26]

The fact is that not only the generalized respect for rules upon which a free-market economy depends but also such indispensable supports as self-discipline, a sense of justice, honesty, fairness, and a responsible concern for the future, must come from beyond the narrowly economic realm.[27] While economic action may sometimes aim at success in satisfying merely selfish desires, the virtue that must be present to some degree before a free market can achieve even this limited goal will exist in society only to the extent that its members are seeking, by acts of ethical will, to restrain merely selfish impulses in favor of those which enrich the common life of all. As Röpke wisely comments,

> the ultimate moral support of the market economy lies outside the market. Market and competition are far

---

25. More, "Definitions of Dualism," 280–81.
26. See *Ibid.*, 252–53. See also Folke Leander, *Inner Check*, 21; 24.
27. Röpke, *Humane Economy*, 125.

from generating their moral prerequisites autono-
mously. This is the error of liberal immanentism. These
prerequisites must be furnished from outside, and it is,
on the contrary, the market and competition which constantly strain them, draw upon them, and consume
them.[28]

---

28. *Ibid.*, 126.

II

The Economic Dimension of Morality

While it is important to recognize with Röpke that "the market economy is not enough," [1] it is equally important not to overlook the essential contribution of economic action to civilized human life. If too many defenders of capitalism have mistakenly seen a sufficient moral basis for the free market in its efficiency alone, other thinkers have erred in the opposite direction by making too sharp a break between efficiency and morality. What this latter group has failed to understand is that, inasmuch as all actions aim at successfully achieving some purpose with the particular means at hand, all actions — including moral actions — are at the same time economic.[2] Some who are accustomed to thinking of the "economic" only in its everyday, pragmatic sense — i.e., as specifically related to material production and exchange — may object to Croce's application of the

---

1. Röpke, *A Humane Economy*, 123.

2. Benedetto Croce, *Philosophy of the Practical: Economic and Ethic* (New York: Biblo and Tannen, 1967; reprint of the original, partly unreliable, English translation), 312–13; 348–50.

term to all purposive actions. Ultimately, however, "economic"refers to the goal of utility which is present in all actions — a point that is recognized by some of the better economists.

Mises notes, for instance, that the "economic principle is a general principle of rational action, and not a specific principle of such action as forms the subject of economic inquiry. The economic principle directs all rational action, all action capable of becoming the subject matter of a science." In a footnote, he adds, "It was left to the empiric–realistic school, with its terrible confusion of all concepts, to explain the economic principle as a specific of production under a money economy." [3]

As Croce has argued persuasively, the difference between merely economic actions and those which are moral is not that the former attempt to achieve efficiency while the latter do not. Nor is the distinction one of "interested" versus "disinterested" actions. In fact, all actions, moral or otherwise, are economic, and all are "interested," since all are directed at achieving a particular purpose envisioned or believed to be desirable by a particular person in a specific set of circumstances.[4] The distinction lies in the *quality* of the end intended. While merely economic actions are directed toward some form of self-indulgence or group imperialism, ethical actions aim at purposes which are simultaneously good for the individual and good for all because inspired by the higher will.

The relationship between the economic and ethical categories of action, Croce explains, is neither one of identity, as held by the utilitarians (the liberal immanentists, in Röpke's terminology), nor of total distinction, as held by those who believe that morality exists in the abstract apart from "interests" of every kind. Instead, the relationship

is that of two degrees, at once distinct and united, such that the first [the economic] can stand without the sec-

3. Mises, *Socialism*, 111–12.

4. Croce, *Philosophy of the Practical*, 349–50.

ond [the ethical], but the second cannot stand without the first. The moment of distinction lies in that possibility of independent existence of the first; the moment of unity is in the impossibility of independent existence of the second. . . . For this reason we have insisted upon showing that there are actions without morality, yet which are perfectly economical, whereas moral actions that are not also perfectly useful or economical do not exist. Morality lives in concrete, in utility, the universal in the individual, the eternal in the contingent.[4a]

In affirming the distinction between the merely economic and the ethical forms of action, says Croce, philosophy does not make use of vague pragmatic classifications such as those used by psychology or economic science (i.e., political economy or economics). He explains that the pragmatic reason used in these fields divides the flow of human experience into somewhat arbitrary classifications which, though useful for certain practical purposes and perfectly legitimate within their own sphere, only approximate the truth. By contrast, philosophy tries to penetrate beyond such merely pragmatic classifications to what is truly universal in experience, to the ultimate categories, or ends, of human action. According to Croce, these include not only the ethical ultimate and the ultimate of efficiency (the economic) but also the ultimates of beauty and truth. Man has a direct, precognitive awareness of these categories through his choosing among these ends. By subsequently reflecting on these acts of valuation, philosophic reason attempts to raise the structure of human experience to clear conceptual awareness — to formulate the universal as it manifests itself in concrete historical actions.

If it were appropriate to use pragmatic or empirical "reason" in making the philosophical distinction between the economic and the ethical forms, writes Croce,

we should doubtless be able to strike the intellect and persuade the soul for a moment, by pointing to the spectacle of life as a demonstration of the two forms, eco-

---

4a. *Ibid.*, 348–49.

nomic and ethic, showing on the one hand, farmers, commercial men, speculators, conquerors of men and of territories, wielders of the word or of the sword as instrument of dominion; and, on the other hand, educators, benefactors, disinterested and self-sacrificing men, martyrs and heroes; on the one hand, economic institutions (manufactories, mines, exchanges, exploration companies), and on the other moral institutions (educators and schools, charitable societies, orders of Sisters of Charity . . .) . . . . However . . . what is touched with the hand is not on that account seized by the intellect, and indeed in a little while it also escapes the hand which had thought to be its master. For when we better observe the individuals who seemed to be merely economic, they seem to be also moral, and inversely; — moral institutions are also economic, and economic moral. The benefactor calculates and wishes to attain his object with the same *cupiditas* as the peasant, all intent upon gain; and the peasant in his turn is ennobled in his chase after lucre by the dignity of labour and by the moral impulses that sustain it; — all charitable institutions are economic undertakings, and economic undertakings are subject to moral laws, so that in drawing up accounts there is no knowing where is that material distinction between the economic and the ethical activities. The truth is that . . . it is not possible to start from contingent facts and from their classes with empirical limitations, to attain to philosophical distinctions, but that it is necessary to start from these, in order to interpret contingent facts, and finally to understand also the mode of formation of empirical classes.[5]

Croce proceeds to describe as "vicious" the results that ensue when merely pragmatic definitions of the economic and the ethical are mistakenly used in situations calling for truly philosophic distinctions[6]; and, indeed, vicious is not too strong a term. Thus, it is wholly legitimate for economists to make no distinction between moral and immoral

5. *Ibid.*, 310–11.
6. *Ibid.*

acts (both of which are economic) *as long as* it is understood that what they are describing is not concrete reality in its fullness but an abstraction from reality which is useful for certain limited, largely quantitative purposes.[7] But it is an entirely different matter when these abstractions masquerade as concrete truth.

What happens then is illustrated, at one extreme, by a verbal exchange that occurred at a 1974 congressional hearing between then-Representative John B. Conlan of Arizona and William C. Norris, chairman of the board and chief operating officer of Control Data Corporation. After Norris acknowledged that several highly sophisticated computers his firm had sold to the Soviet and Polish governments could be put to military use, Conlan said he found it hard to understand a businessman wanting to "sell that type of equipment to an opposing state which has indicated. . . that they want to take control of the world and us in the process." When Conlan then asked Norris if making such sales bothered him "at night when you go to sleep," Norris replied: "Of course not. If it did, I wouldn't do it." Besides, he added, such sales were allowed by governmental policy. Conlan then asked: "[I]f the government says it's all right, then you don't have any further questions of conscience about anything?" To which Norris — true to the notion that morality is completely separate from economic matters — responded that, "Certainly," he had a conscience, "but on the other hand, somebody has to make decisions and my conscience is not too relevant. . . . I am not a politician. I am not a theologian. I am a businessman."[8] At another extreme, the acceptance of arbitrary or superficial definitions of the economic form as fully descriptive of reality has led many, in reaction, to draw a false distinction between political freedom (usually seen as noble

---

7. See *Ibid.*, Second Part, First Section, Chapter V.

8. This incident was witnessed by the present writer. For a fuller account, see "How Control Data Corp. 'Justifies' Red Trade," *Human Events*, Vol. XXXIV, No. 21 (May 25, 1974), 5.

and therefore desirable) and economic freedom (seen as base, hence unimportant).

Once it is realized that, from the standpoint of philosophy proper, every action is an economic action and all actions are subject to the moral obligation, it follows that economic and political freedom are philosophically indistinguishable. Hence, to ask what kind of economic order is most compatible with man's higher purpose is to ask the same question regarding the political order and vice versa. In the remaining pages, we shall see that the Babbittian–Crocean [9] definition of morality in terms of will (i.e., practical action) rather than preconceived intellectual blueprints has far-reaching implications for the proper ordering of the world's politico–economic systems.

---

9. Burke also conceives of morality in this way. See Joseph F. Baldacchino, Jr., "The Value-Centered Historicism of Edmund Burke," *Modern Age*, XXVII (Spring 1983).

III

Economics As Means to Morality

The view that the ultimate moral standard is a supra-individual quality of will whose intrinsic goal transcends the merely selfish and arbitrary, differs from an older Western tendency of thought with some roots in the classical and Christian heritage, which is to associate the universal moral order with abstract intellectual precepts or norms of conduct. Commenting on this largely static notion of morality, Ryn observes:

> The belief that true justice in the individual and society requires the imitation of a pre-existing intellectual model of perfection tends to treat individuality as such as unimportant. This belief breeds suspicion of the view that government and society in general should try to accommodate diverse competing interests. Must not the moral approach be simply to disregard particular interests and to implement the disinterested moral blueprint? [1]

---

1. Claes G. Ryn, "History and the Moral Order," in Francis J. Canavan, ed. *The Ethical Dimension of Political Life* (Durham: Duke University Press, 1983), 102.

By contrast, the concept of universal morality as a special form of practical action having the universal good as its end more fully corresponds to the historical and dynamic nature of human life. According to this view, morality does not involve mechanical imitation of a pre-existing normative pattern somehow known in advance by human reason (which to be completely reliable would require human omniscience). Rather, morality is seen as the creative ordering of the potentialities inherent in particular circumstances in such a way as to promote the good of all. And since circumstances are infinitely varied and constantly changing, men are forever faced with the necessity of making new moral choices — but always with a view to the one unchanging moral end.

Compared with a more rationalistic view of morality, the voluntarist approach displays a greater awareness of the contribution that diverse individuals — with their unique talents, varied perspectives, and different kinds and degrees of knowledge — can bring to the enrichment of their common existence. To take advantage of this potential, a society informed by such an ethical view will tend toward a decentralized politico–economic system — one having numerous competing centers of authority and allowing sufficient scope for the citizenry to pursue a vast array of intellectual, aesthetic, economic and ethical activities. Aware that the good can be advanced in myriad ways and that it is sometimes impossible to perceive whether good or evil has been served by particular actions until considerable time has elapsed, a society will be characterized by a high degree of individual freedom. In a sense, therefore, a politico–economic order of this kind could be described as individualistic. But since man's search for his own true humanity is also a profoundly cooperative effort involving not only those who live now but the contributions of those who have died, it would be highly inaccurate to portray society in the atomistic terms favored by nineteenth-century liberalism and its contemporary intellectual progeny.

To the extent that society has as its purpose the promotion of man's higher good, its basic point of reference will not be the abstract individual conceived in isolation from all the relationships and obligations that constitute and make his life worthwhile. Instead, a society of this kind will comprise real persons living and working within a network of spontaneously formed and overlapping interpersonal associations, such as the family, church, workplace, labor union, neighborhood, and so on. It is within such "autonomous groups," as Robert Nisbet has pointed out,[2] that individuals develop their essential human nature.

Nisbet stresses that it is in the context of these small groups — where men's everyday actions can have noticeable effects on their own lives and the lives of those around them — that men find friendship, affection, recognition and the incentives to work and love, which only later are projected outward to society at large. Most importantly, such mediating structures — particularly the family, church and school — provide a major source of inspiration for the difficult task of moral character building without reference to which all discussion of peace, justice, and human brotherhood at the national or international level is substantively meaningless.[3]

Beyond the support provided by its mediating structures, a society whose members are striving for true community will find additional and related sources of ethical inspiration in literature, art, and tradition. The latter, as Walter Lippmann noted a generation ago, constitutes

the public world to which our private worlds are joined.

2. See Robert A. Nisbet, *The Quest for Community* (London: Oxford University Press, 1953).

3. For a more detailed discussion of the difference between true community and sentimental notions of abstract human brotherhood, see Claes G. Ryn, "The Things of Caesar: Notes Toward the Delimitation of Politics," *Thought*, Vol. 55, No. 219 (December 1980). See also Claes G. Ryn, "The Work of Community," in Philip F. Lawler, ed. *Papal Economics* (Washington, D.C.: Heritage Foundation, 1981). This issue is also treated in depth in Irving Babbitt, *Rousseau and Romanticism* (Austin: University of Texas Press, 1977), esp. Chapters 4 and 5.

> This continuum of public and private memories transcends all persons in their immediate and natural lives and it ties them all together. In it there is performed the mystery by which individuals are adopted and initiated into membership in the community.
>
> The body which carries this mystery is the history of the community, and its central theme is the great deeds and the high purposes of the great predecessors. From them the new men descend and prove themselves by becoming participants in the unfinished story.

Lippmann goes on to observe that it is by ordering his natural impulses according to the higher standard partially embodied in history and tradition that the individual becomes civilized.[4] Of course, not all deeds embodied in history are inspired by noble motives; in fact, quite the contrary. Hence, the good society will not cling blindly to a rigid traditionalism — which would suggest the "story" were, indeed, finished — but will continually subject present beliefs and norms to critical re-evaluation with reference to what is directly known of the transcendent purpose they are supposed to advance.[5]

Related to this on-going evaluation and renewal of tradition is the effort to formulate particular rules for the governing of conduct. Such rules or precepts are indispensable in the life of any society. Their value derives, however, from their usefulness in serving some purpose. While the purposes thus served can be either ethical or merely utilitarian, it can be said that in a society whose members are striving toward genuine civilization such rules will frequently be formulated with a view to man's higher needs.[6] What is here said about rules and principles of con-

---

4. Walter Lippmann, *The Public Philosophy* (New York: New American Library, 1955), 105.

5. Ryn, *Democracy and the Ethical Life*, 87–88.

6. It should be noted here that, as the requirements of the ethical will change with circumstances, even norms of conduct that are formulated with genuine sensitivity to the demands of morality are at best pragmatic guidelines for action which must be transcended in the moment of actual choice by the needs of the particular situation. See Ryn, "History and the Moral Order," 100–101.

duct applies not only to laws and regulations enforced by governmental bodies but also to the various principles formulated by economists and widely followed, such as (to name just one example) that free trade is preferable to protectionist policies. Insofar as the effects of following free-trade policies, e.g., a higher material standard of living for the populace, are approved as conducive to the highest ends of society, such a principle serves not only an economic purpose but also universal morality. To the extent, however, that the higher end requires that other needs be taken into account (e.g., national security, as in the case of the Control Data Corporation's computer sales cited earlier), then morality would dictate that the principle favoring free trade must be supplemented by some other principle, as, for example, that it will be illegal or unethical to provide sustenance to an enemy government whose intentions are known to be evil. That it is common in everyday empirical language to describe the first principle mentioned as "economic" and the second as "political" or "moral" is irrelevant to philosophy. Both principles are moral to the extent they serve the universal good and immoral to the extent they do not.[7]

Now it is a matter of record that, in their actual historical development, the various politico–economic systems generally described as democratic and capitalist (such as those in the United States, Canada and the Western European nations) have conformed in some considerable measure to the conditions of the good society just outlined. In general, it is not abstract economic man — each individual an island unto himself pursuing his own narrowly conceived self-interest — who has used and enjoyed the unparalleled freedom available in these countries. It has been used by fathers, mothers, aunts, uncles, teachers, priests, artists, union members, volunteer firemen, Knights of Columbus, Little League coaches. Each has obligations

---

7. See Croce, *Philosophy of the Practical, passim.*

beyond himself — to family, friends, employees, co-workers, ultimately to civilization — and these, more than anything, give meaning to his life (though it must be remembered that the temptation to evade these responsibilities is always strong; morality is not easy).

When businessmen strive to save a struggling company, is nothing involved other than arbitrary self-interest such as greed or lust for power? Sometimes yes, and in those instances no morality is present. Other times, however — perhaps far more often than is realized by those who reflexively belittle all things "economic" or "bourgeois" — such a struggle can represent the will to the higher good of all affected. For instance, a seemingly selfish company president may be trying to save his company for the sake of securing jobs and indirectly perhaps a whole community with all of what it entails of religious, ethical, educational, and cultural activities.

We might add that, even when narrow self-interest *is* the motive for action, it can in favorable circumstances be enlisted in the service of the higher good by the ethical forces in the surrounding community, which subject selfishness to a degree of control. Ryn notes, for example, that "a businessman concerned only with his own well-being and pleasure and trying to make a profit to further that end may under certain cultural circumstances still help to advance a higher goal. Provided that the market demand to which he is responding is itself cultured and at least partially due to a wish on the part of the buyers to realize moral ends, the businessman's desire to make a profit, which is the reward for having served the consumer efficiently, may actually give some support to the ethical life of society. In spite of the low moral quality of his own ultimate motive, higher goals are served by his economic risk taking and imagination." [8] Ryn's point is not that businessmen are necessarily selfish. But even when they *are* selfish, economic motives

---

8. *Democracy and the Ethical Life*, 86.

can under favorable social and cultural conditions have ethically beneficial practical effects.[9]

It is a mistake to think of the institution of private property as it has evolved in the Western democracies as a narrowly economic phenomenon useful for earning money and building financial empires but unrelated to man's moral and social nature. Private property should instead be viewed as means which can be used either by the lower will for arbitrary purposes or by the higher will to advance the universal good. In the former case, its use is merely economic; in the latter, it is both economic and ethical, which is to say that not only utility is willed but utility in the service of an end which is intrinsically good.

That it is simplistic to think of private ownership only in economic terms, and not also in terms of its potential for serving man's higher purpose, becomes more obvious when it is realized that to speak of private property is but shorthand for saying that the freedom to make effective choices, which requires some control over resources, is spread widely among the citizens in their freely formed associations, rather than being monopolized by the centralized administrative apparatus of the total state.

In short, private property is synonymous with freedom; hence, what Burke said of freedom is equally true of private property: it should be promoted and safeguarded by government to the extent that it serves the higher good but restricted to the extent it is abused (i.e., put to demeaning, destructive use). And since the proper balance depends upon the (ever-changing) "character and circumstances" of the people to be governed, it is impossible to determine in the abstract the exact manner and extent to which the use of such property should be protected, rather than re-

---

9. Of course, the same question of motives that is here applied to businessmen is equally relevant to intellectuals (is truth really sought, or is it sacrificed in favor of unmerited recognition or some other unworthy purpose?), artists (is life portrayed in its fullness, or are essential aspects left out?), and all other groups.

stricted, by the state.[10] But though there is no absolute
right to property in the way that many have argued in the
abstract manner of Locke, far more dangerous is the notion, fostered by Marxists and others, which holds that all
authority and all resources to shape new reality should be
centralized in the state. Instead, we can say of property
rights what Burke said of historical rights in general: they
"are in a sort of middle." [11]

While it is impossible to define in advance the specific
extent to which private property is justified (since this
depends on circumstances), what can be said, given the
above-noted importance of mediating structures (hence
decentralization of authority and resources) to man's moral
and social development, is that the good society will always
display a high level of respect for private property in some
form.[12]

Though private property, free markets and the wide-
spread distribution of economic resources have provided
crucial support to man's higher disposition, their contribution to man's ethical development has frequently been over-
looked by individualistic liberalism. Without both the
relative freedom and control of resources needed to act
effectively, institutions lying intermediate to the individual
and the state — family, church, local community — would be
functionally impotent and incapable of contributing ade-
quately to man's moral and social growth. But when the
principles of modern liberalism were first being developed
two centuries ago, these bodies were so strong that their

---

10. See Edmund Burke, *Reflections on the Revolution in France*, ed.
Conor Cruise O'Brien (Harmondsworth: Penguin Books, 1969), 151.

11. *Ibid.*, 153.

12. It might be pointed out that respect for rules protecting
property, like respect for behavioral norms in general, derives neither
from the intrinsic worth of those rules, as various schools of abstract,
natural-right theory tend to believe, nor from their usefulness in maxi-
mizing some aggregate of merely economic self-interest, as held by
Hayek in common with the utilitarians. Instead, such rules will ultimately
be respected precisely to the extent that they are perceived as supporting
man's higher, or ethical, purpose.

effects on the moral development of the individual were largely taken for granted. As Nisbet observes,

> What we can now see with the advantage of hindsight is that, unconsciously, the founders of liberalism abstracted certain moral and psychological attributes from a *social organization* and considered these the timeless, natural qualities of the *individual*, who was regarded as independent of the influences of any historically developed social organization. Those qualities that, in their entirety, composed the eighteenth-century liberal image of man were qualities actually inhering to a large extent in a set of institutions and groups, all of which were aspects of historical tradition.[13]

This failure of insight has led to numerous unfortunate consequences. One is a tendency on the part of modern liberalism (in common with various collectivist ideologies) increasingly to give to the centralized state, usually under the guise of helping individuals, functions that historically belonged to man's more intimate groups. The result is to deprive these groups of true functional importance, thereby draining them of the authority and emotional significance without which they are powerless to perform their essential socializing role. What then happens is vividly illustrated by George Gilder's recent description of the havoc wreaked on lower-income families by misguided welfare programs.[14]

It has long been recognized, says Gilder, that "welfare was harsh on intact poor families," but until recently it was thought that the problem lay in policies that required the absence of the father before benefits would be extended to the remainder of the family. However, when an experimental program in twenty-six states newly provided benefits to families having unemployed fathers living at home, it was discovered that the change "had no effect on the rate at

---

13. Nisbet, *Quest for Community*, 225–26.

14. By drawing on Gilder's argument, we are not implying the deleterious effect of all welfare programs but seeking to illustrate the intimate connection between ethics and economics.

which poor families broke down." Why? "The reason was clear," writes Gilder. The "marriages dissolve not because the rules dictate it, but because the benefit levels destroy the father's key role and authority." Also destroyed for the father are many of the incentives for moral effort.[15]

While the father's position as provider formerly was a source of "male confidence and authority," says Gilder, affording him "respect from the wife and children and motivation to face the tedium and frustration of daily labor," nothing

> is so destructive to all these male values as the growing, imperious recognition that when all is said and done his wife and children can do better without him. The man has the gradually sinking feeling that his role as provider, the definitive male activity from the primal days of the hunt through the industrial revolution and on into modern life has been largely seized from him; he has been cuckolded by the compassionate state.
>
> His response to this reality is that very combination of resignation and rage, escapism and violence, short horizons and promiscuous sexuality that characterizes everywhere the life of the poor. But in this instance, the pattern is not so much a necessary reflection of economic conditions as an arbitrary imposition of policy — a policy that by depriving poor families of strong fathers both dooms them to poverty and damages the economic prospects of the children.
>
> In the welfare culture money becomes not something earned by men through hard work, but a right conferred on women by the state. Protests and complaint replace diligence and discipline as the sources of pay. Boys grow up seeking support from women, while they find manhood in the macho circles of the street and the bar or in the irresponsible fathering of random progeny.[16]

---

15. George Gilder, *Wealth and Poverty* (New York: Bantam Books, 1981), 139.

16. *Ibid.*, 139–40.

Beyond its failure to recognize the important ethical role played by intermediate groups — a role that is undermined when policy is made as though society were "simply a numerical aggregate" of "discrete and socially separated" individuals [17] — *laissez-faire* liberalism has also tended to ascribe to a mere lack of economic perspicacity actions on the part of collectivist rulers that should more accurately be viewed as stemming from arbitrary, hence immoral, motives. We earlier referred, for example, to Mises' demonstration that the economic calculation necessary for an efficient allocation of resources is impossible in the absence of free markets and private ownership of property. It must now be pointed out, however, that from a strictly philosophic viewpoint Mises' account is questionable.

Mises begins by noting that the "essential mark of socialism is that *one will* alone [either that of a single individual or of a small, tightly knit politburo] acts. . . . One will alone chooses, decides, directs, acts, gives orders. All the rest simply obey orders and instructions." He then concedes that the ruler or rulers may be "people of superior ability, wise and full of good intentions." But, he says, without the price signals provided by the spontaneous order of the unhampered market — an order which springs naturally from the willingness of all men to exchange what they value less for what they value more — the socialist ruler will have no way of calculating the relative costs and outputs of various combinations of resources (virtually infinite in number and constantly changing) which are potentially useful in carrying out his own economic plan. "Our problem, the crucial and only problem of socialism," Mises writes, "is a purely economic problem, and as such refers merely to means and not to ultimate ends." [18]

The underlying assumption here, of course, is that the collectivist rulers are seriously interested in achieving the goals enumerated in their published plans, which usually

---

17. Nisbet, *Quest for Community*, 249.
18. Mises, *Human Action*, 695–97; emphasis in original.

promise greater material well-being for the masses. As Croce knew, however, actions speak louder than words.[19] Hence, the fact that the rulers continue to impose a centralized politico–economic structure, even at the expense of failing year after year to fulfill their promises to the people, indicates quite simply that what they really value most is not the goals published for public consumption but the gratification to their own egos that comes from wielding immense power while claiming to act for the people.

Contrary to Mises, the only ones free to act without undue external interference in such a society — the small group of rulers — are indeed engaging in rational economic calculation: they are sacrificing what they value less (the common good) to what they value more (their own power and the resulting flattery to their egos). What Mises might have said — but did not since he lacked the philosophic distinction between good and evil will [20] — is that, by depriving its citizens of adequate opportunities, including economic means, for work contributing to real community, the fully

---

19. See Croce, *Philosophy of the Practical*, esp. 53–56.

20. Adam Smith, who was the first systematic explicator of free-market principles and is widely regarded as the father of economics, had a far more advanced conception of man's moral nature than is widely assumed. Smith writes that man has a "natural sense of duty" — significantly involving more than mere utility — which, though precognitive, is "afterwards confirmed by reasoning and philosophy." He goes on to note that our moral faculties "were set up within us to be the supreme arbiters of all our actions, to superintend all our senses, passions, and appetites, and to judge how far each of them was either to be indulged or restrained.... The very words, right, wrong, fit, improper, graceful, unbecoming, mean only what pleases or displeases those faculties." By "acting according to the dictates of our moral faculties," Smith adds, "we necessarily pursue the most effectual means for promoting the happiness of mankind, and may therefore be said, in some sense, to cooperate with the Deity, and to advance, as far as in our power, the plan of providence. By acting otherwise, on the contrary, we seem to obstruct, in some measure, the scheme which the Author of Nature has established for the happiness and perfection of the world, and to declare ourselves... in some measure the enemies of God." See Adam Smith, *The Theory of Moral Sentiments* (New Rochelle, N.Y.: Arlington House, 1969), 232–35; 270–71; 276–77.

centralized state conflicts in the most essential way with the requirements of man's moral nature.

By giving inadequate consideration to the relationship between economics and the moral order, then, some of the free-market system's most illustrious champions have failed to demonstrate its true moral worth while prematurely conceding to collectivist planners "good intentions." In the great contest for the world, the intellectual leaders of the West clearly must present a more comprehensive vision of reality than the one offered by various forms of economistic liberalism — a vision that takes into account the ethical imperatives of human nature. When viewed from this perspective, the free-market system — with its wide diffusion of private property within a context of limited government — can be seen as a highly fruitful condition for the pursuit of man's ethical and spiritual ends.[21]

---

21. While the arguments advanced in the current work are intended to appeal to general experience and not to dogmas peculiar to particular religious bodies, it is nevertheless true that the conclusions reached here have many parallels in Catholic social teaching from Pope Leo XIII through Pope John Paul II. See Pope Leo XIII, Encyclical "Rerum Novarum" (1891), esp. Nos. 7–11, 17–18, 20–22, 27–28, 35–36, 45–46, 51–55, 71–72; Pope Pius XI, Encyclical "Quadragesimo Anno" (1931), esp. Nos. 42–49, 78–81, 88; Pope John Paul II, Encyclical "Laborem Exercens" (1981), esp. Nos. 6–7, 8–10, 12–14.

Index

Action, categories of, 16
Aristotle, 17
Art: as source of community, 31

Babbitt, Irving, 9, 17, 18n, 31n
Baldacchino, Joseph, 9, 12, 28n
Burke, Edmund, 28n, 35, 36

Capitalism, defined, 13n; dependence
    on higher order, 13
Catholic social teaching, 41n
Charity, 11
Collectivism: fully centralized state
    conflicts with morality, 39–41
Community: distinguished from
    abstract brotherhood, 31
Conlan, John B., 27
Control Data Corporation, 27, 33
Croce, Benedetto: on distinction
    between pragmatic and philo-
    sophic reason, 25; on relation
    between the economic and the
    ethical, 24–26; on the ultimate
    categories of action, 25; men-
    tioned, 17, 40

Economic freedom: indistinguishable
    from political freedom, 28

Efficiency, relation to morality,
    23–28
Engels, Friedrich, 15n
Envy, 11
Ethical conscience, defined, 18–19, 20

Fortitude, 11
Free-enterprise system, 13
Free-market system: as support for
    morality, 41; mentioned, 13

Generosity, 12
Gilder, George, 37–38

Haag, Ernest van den, 14n
Happiness: distinguished from
    pleasure, 21
Hayek, Friedrich A.: does not
    acknowledge transcendent moral
    purpose, 15–16; mentioned, 17,
    20, 36n
Higher will, defined, 17–18, 19
Honesty, necessity of in advanced
    economy, 10–11
Human Events, 27n

Individualism, deficiency of atomistic
    view, 30
Industria, 11

John Paul II, Pope, 41n

Kirk, Russell: on deficiencies of economistic liberalism, 16–17; on libertarians, 17

"Laborem Exercens" (Encyclical), 41n
Laissez-faire liberalism, deficiency of, 17, 30–31, 33–37, 39, 41
Lawler, Philip F., 31n
Leander, Folke, 17, 18n
Leo XIII, Pope, 41n
Lippmann, Walter, 31–32
Literature: as source of community, 31
Lower will, defined, 17–18, 19

Market economy, need for virtue in, 10–12, 21–22
Marx, Karl, 14
Marxism and Marxists, 11, 13, 36
Mediating structures, 31
Mill, John Stuart, 20–21
Mises, Ludwig von, moral relativism of, 15, 39–40; mentioned, 9, 17, 19, 24
Modern Age, 17n, 28n
Morality: as abstract intellectual precepts, deficiency of, 29; as special quality of will, 29–30; economic dimension of, 23–28
More, Paul Elmer, 17, 18n, 21

Nisbet, Robert A.: on autonomous groups, 31, 37; mentioned, 39n

Norris, William C., 27
Novak, Michael, 17n

Pius XI, Pope, 41n
Pleasure: distinguished fom happiness, 21
Political freedom: indistinguishable from economic freedom, 28
Precepts, provisional nature of, 32–33, 36
Property: as condition for morality, 35–37, 41; as freedom, 36–37

"Quadragesimo Anno" (Encyclical), 41n

"Rerum Novarum" (Encyclical), 41n
Rigid traditionalism, deficiency of, 32
Röpke, Wilhelm: on Communism, 14; on relation of economic system to wider moral order, 13–14, 17, 21–22, 23, 24; mentioned, 9–10
Ryn, Claes G., 17, 18, 19–20, 29, 31n

Self interest: can support higher good, 19, 34–35; insufficiency in narrow sense, 34
Smith, Adam, 40n
Socialism: fully centralized state conflicts with morality, 39–41

Thought, 31n
Tradition, 31–32

Will, categories of, 16